ShrinkLits

ShrinkLits

**Seventy of the
world's towering classics
cut down to size**

by Maurice Sagoff

**Illustrations by
Roslyn Schwartz**

Revised and expanded edition

**Workman Publishing
New York**

Library of Congress Cataloging in Publication Data

Sagoff, Maurice.
   ShrinkLits: seventy of the world's towering classics
cut down to size.

   I. Title.
PS3569.A36S5   1980   811'.54   79-56532
ISBN 0-89480-079-5

Cover Design: Paul Hanson
Cover Illustration: Roslyn Schwartz
Book Design: Florence Mayers

Workman Publishing Company, Inc.
1 West 39 Street
New York, New York 10018

Manufactured in the United States of America
First Printing April 1980

10 9 8 7 6 5 4

Dedication

For Sara and Mark
and Charlotte

Contents

Introduction

The world of books is in horrendous
turmoil—booklovers, students, and readers in
general are simply unable to keep up with the
ceaseless flow of new titles while still devoting some
precious time to the older classics.

With all this weighty agglomeration of literary
timber, it is a fact that inside every fat book is a
skinny book trying to get out, struggling to cut
through the mummylike wrappings of long-winded
descriptions, superfluous characters, endless
conversations, and turgid style, striving to emerge
new-minted and succinct, the quintessence of the
work in which it had been unhappily confined.

Putting these two scenarios together, we can readily
see that our literary salvation depends on our
making less and less of more and more. In other
words, one can get to be a well-rounded reader only
through well-flattened books. How to achieve this
had been a vexing problem until the development of
the *ShrinkLit* process whereby books undergo a
kind of constructive distillation which boils out the
fat and renders the meat (so to speak) into verse,
making it at once more lucid and palatable. And, of
course, the results are extremely energy-saving and
cost-effective.

A word about the choice of works in this revised,
updated sampling. When the first edition of
ShrinkLits flashed across the literary horizon ten

years ago, readers were quick to suggest their favorite classics for treatment, but not always was the matter taken seriously. "How about this, for the *Complete Works of Henry Miller*," wrote one wag: "Henry Miller has a callus/On his phallus." Since I have attempted to keep within the bounds of propriety, such offerings were, of course, disregarded. Another enthusiast suggested that the reductive process be intensified by shrinking two books together, say, *The Joy of Cooking* and *The Joy of Sex* into one. This proved to be impractical, with so many mixing instructions; and the notion was discarded. Suffice it to say that the seventy examples in this little volume were written with an eye to the typical home library, with the hope that the reader may be inspired to carry on this conservation effort, for personal pleasure and profit.

Maurice Sagoff

Preface ShrinkLit: Elements of Style

William Strunk, Jr. and E. B. White

"Omit needless words!"
Said Strunk to White.

"You're right,"
Said White,
"That's nice
Advice,
But Strunk,
You're drunk
With words —
Two-thirds
Of those
You chose
For that
Fiat
Would fill
The bill!

Would not
The thought
— The core —
Be more
Succinct
If shrinked
(Or shrunk)?"

Said Strunk:
"Good grief!
I'm brief
(I thought)
P'raps not . . .
Dear me!
Let's see . . .
Okay!
Just say
'Write tight!'
No fat
in that!"

"Quite right!"
Said White,
"Er — I mean 'Quite!'
Or, simply, 'Right!' "

ShrinkLits

Moll Flanders
Daniel Defoe

*The Fortunes and Misfortunes of the famous
Moll Flanders, who was born in Newgate, and
during a life of continued variety, for
threescore years, besides her childhood,
was twelve years a Whore, five times
a Wife (thereof once to her own
brother), twelve years a
thief, eight years a
transported Felon in Virginia,
at last grew rich, lived honest,
and died a penitent.
Written from her
own Memorandums.*

—Original Title Page

That's the story,
  Briefly told.

At age 70,
  Weak and old,

Pricked by conscience,
  Moll retires,

Banks her savings
  And her fires;

She repents her
  Sins and all . . .

Love your sense of timing,
  Moll.

The Courtship of Miles Standish
Henry Wadsworth Longfellow

Standish, not a
    Lady-killer,
Bids John Alden
    Woo Priscilla
For him. She is
    Not put on:
"Why not do your
    Own thing, John?"

Plights are trothed
    Or troths are plighted
(Or whatever
    Those benighted
Times demanded
    Of true lovers)
Soon they're snuggled
    'Twixt the covers . . .

Smiling bravely,
    Standish mumbles
"Thus it is
    Ye cookie crumbles."

Beowulf

Monster Grendel's tastes are plainish.
Breakfast? Just a couple Danish.

King of Danes is frantic, very.
Wait! Here comes the Malmö ferry

Bringing Beowulf, his neighbor,
Mighty swinger with a saber!

Hrothgar's warriors hail the Swede,
Knocking back a lot of mead;

Then, when night engulfs the Hall
And the Monster makes his call,

Beowulf, with body-slam
Wrenches off his arm, Shazam!

Monster's mother finds him slain,
Grabs and eats another Dane!

Down her lair our hero jumps,
Gives old Grendel's dam her lumps.

Later on, as king of Geats
He performed prodigious feats

Till he met a foe too tough
(Non-Beodegradable stuff)

And that scaly-armored dragon
Scooped him up and fixed his wagon.

Sorrow-stricken, half the nation
Flocked to Beowulf's cremation;
Round his pyre, with drums a-muffle
Did a Nordic soft-shoe shuffle.

The Pied Piper of Hamelin
Robert Browning

Town made
    Rat free!
Unpaid
    Piper, he
Pipes kids
    Into hills.
Weird fate!
    Moral: Pay
Your bills,
    Cheapskate.

Babbitt
Sinclair Lewis

He'd slap your back
    And raise your gorge,
But gosh, what a
    Promoter! George
Could sell an Eskimo
    A Norge.

A cliché-ridden
    Business nit,
He cheated, boozed
    And bragged a bit,
Said "Okeydoke"
    "Crissakes," "Hot Spit!"

Ordained to lead
    The booboisie,
He sensed his med-
    Iocrity,
And told son Ted,
    "Don't be like me."

Ah, quaint old days
    When Dads could tell
Their offspring "Go—
    Dissent, rebel!"
He did it, though
    It hurt like hell.

He proved by this
    Apostasy
That George, despite
    His Babbittry
Was not a dud.
    Not totally.

Frankenstein
Mary Shelley

In his occult-science lab
Frankenstein creates a flab
Which, endowed with human will,
Very shortly starts to kill.
First, it pleads a lonely life
And demands a monster-wife;
"Monstrous!" Frankenstein objects,
Thinking of the side-effects.

Chilled with fear, he quits the scene,
But the frightful man-machine
Follows him in hot pursuit
Bumping people off *en route*,
Till at last it stands, malign,
By the corpse of Frankenstein!

Somewhere in the northern mists
— Horrid thing — *it still exists* . . .
Still at large, a-thirst for gore!
Got a strong lock on your door?

Metamorphosis
Franz Kafka

Gregor Samsa wakes to find
He's a bug — the cockroach kind,
But it's really not surprising,
Life's been so dehumanizing —
Lack of meaning, warmth and joy
Bugged him since he was a boy.

Now in monstrous insect shape
Still unable to escape,
He takes refuge on the ceiling
Which exacerbates the feeling
Of the household. Papa shies
Apples at him. Mother cries.
(Parents should receive their due
But "My son, the cockroach?" Fooh!)
Next, the servants try to scat him,
Sister plays her fiddle at him —
Nothing helps. He pines. He dies . . .
Presto! All the family ties
Seem to strengthen; no one glooms,
Sister actually blooms!
Vulgar selfish life resumes.

(If you crave interpretation
Of the Kafkaesque relation
To the world of man and mind,
Critics say it's best defined
As: "Gnostic-Manichaean, in the sense that the
Absolute here, as a pure origin of Being, is
just as powerless in its transcendent remoteness
as it is inaccessible, whereas the earthly creation
is basically one of dreariness and corruption.")

So. Excuse the interruption.

Dr. Jekyll and Mr. Hyde

Robert Louis Stevenson

In his nature
　　Two halves vied —
Gentle Jekyll,
　　Beastly Hyde,
Struggling each
　　To get outside.

He cooked up a
　　Potent brew,
When he drank it,
　　Switcheroo!
What resulted
　　Scared him, too.

Had he been a
　　Smarter doc
He'd have scooted
　　Round the block
To the Mental
　　Health Assoc.

They'd have had him
　　Analyzed
(Schizoid type,
　　Externalized).
Then, his psyche
　　Normalized,

Traumas would be
　　Transitory,
Gone would be the
　　Details gory!
And loused-up
　　A nifty story.

Around the World in Eighty Days
Jules Verne

Phileas Fogg
    A wager lays
To round the earth
    In eighty days!
With Passepartout
    Through storm and heat
This cool cat comes
    On little Fogg feet;
He wins the bet
    And weds, to boot,
The maid he snatched
    From death *en route*.

Thrills, chills and spills
    At every turn!
Like something out of
    Say, Jules Verne.

Kubla Khan
Samuel Taylor Coleridge

In Xanadu
    (Near north Iran)
A fun-house built
    By Kubla Khan
Had founts of gold
    And curvilinear
Damsels fresh
    From Abyssinia!
(Thus dreamed Coleridge,
    Snug in bed,
Opium coursing
    Through his head);
Just when all the
    Vibes were zinging
And the dulcimers
    Were winging,
Plonk! Some guy
    With goods to sell
Knocked! and broke
    The poet's spell. . .

Curse the clumsy
    Thoughtless lout!
Just a sneaky
    Narc, no doubt;
Faugh! the thought
    Leaves one disgusted —
Here's a *poem*
    Being busted!

The Catcher in the Rye
J. D. Salinger

School was crummy,
    Classmates mean,
Holden Caulfield,
    Aged sixteen,
Dropped out to the New York scene.

There he wandered,
    Sorrow's son,
Overgrown
    But underdone,
Seared by girls . . . it wasn't fun.

Broke, disheartened,
    Home he slid,
Sister Phoebe,
    (Perky kid),
Buoyed him up, she really did.

Only for the
    Moment, though;
Down the skids
    Alas, he'll go,
Landing in a shrink château.

Ah, what torment
    Must be his
Who Goddamns
    But feels Gee Whiz!
Youth is rough — it really is.

Oliver Twist
Charles Dickens

Workhouse orphan
    Asks more gruel—
Zap! He's out.
    The world is cruel.
Bad guys, Fagin,
    Sikes and such,
Keep him in a
    Frightful clutch;
Good guys help him
    Doggedly,
Seeking his
    Identity . . .

Secret papers—
    Wills, a ring—
It's a compli-
    Cated thing,
Sentimental,
    Overdrawn,
Corny; but it
    Might catch on
As a musical,
    A show,
Or a film—
    You never know.

34

Inferno
Dante Alighieri

Like a funky show?
Like your torture slow?
Come on down below!

See historic greats,
Thugs and reprobates
Suffer hellish fates;

Filth around them laves
Hear them in their caves
Screaming "Don't make waves!"

Using all the tricks
Of the horror flicks,
Dante feeds us kicks.

Sure, a moral's there:
"Godless man, beware!"
Heard that tune somewhere?

Antigone
Sophocles

Tyrant Creon's stern advice is
"Do not bury Polynices!
Thebes' defenders had to squash him —
Now we'll let the buzzards nosh him!"
But Antigone, the brave,
Dared to dig her brother's grave:
"Man-made laws my soul defies —
Live by laws divine!" she cries.

Creon locks her up, the demon!
Though she's pledged to marry Haemon
(That's his son). Now comes a seer
Prophesying woes severe:
If her brother's not entombed
And she dies, then Haemon's doomed!

Creon, seeing things go screwy,
Wilts, and tries to bang a U-ee,
But the Gods who drive the hearse
Seldom shove it in reverse . . .
Carnage follows, sure as Fate;
Here's the body-count to date —
1. Antigone 2. her brother
3. young Haemon 4. his mother
(If more bodies fail to fall,
It's because the cast is small).

Strung-out Creon takes the blame,
Exits, croaking "Rotten shame!"

King Lear
William Shakespeare

Daughters three had agèd Lear,
Two were rotten, one sincere.

He misjudged the loving kid,
Cursed and cut her off, he did.

But the others, flushed with gain,
Tossed him out into the rain.

All his ganglia came untied;
Sweet Cordelia reached his side

Just too late to change the play—
Overkill was underway:

Lear succumbed, and all his girls,
Plus his fool and various earls.
———
Ah, if but the womb would breed
Kind, sincere and loving seed

Full of filial thoughtfulness,
None would perish in distress;

Heaven on earth this life would be!
Folks would die of sheer ennui.

Silas Marner

George Eliot

Lonely codger
    Gets a peppy
Little lodger,
    Foundling Eppie.
"Eppie in de
    Toal hole" bugs him;
She's a rascal
    But she hugs him,
Thaws his spirit,
    He stops brooding,
Makes new friendships
    (Not including
Twenty million
    High school students
Who by choice
    Or through imprudence
Had to make a
    Book report of
Silas Marner)—

That's fame . . .
    Sort of.

The Rime of the Ancient Mariner

Samuel Taylor Coleridge

Aged pest
    Buttonholes
Wedding guest,
    Rigmaroles
How bird
    Hexed boat;
Prayer kept
    Him afloat.
"Love conquers all"
    Unquote.

Uncle Tom's Cabin
Harriet Beecher Stowe

Poor blacks in shacks
    (Tom and the likes)
Raise psalms, not arms
    When "Massa" strikes.

Appease Legrees?
    Tom gets the whip.
Grim thought: Did not
    This slave precip-
Itate the fate
    He suffered from
By being such
    An Uncle Tom?

Rip Van Winkle
Washington Irving

In the Catskills
    Rip, a drifter,
Meets wee keglers,
    Takes a snifter
(Borscht it isn't)
    Down he goes
For a zwanzig-jahre
    Doze . . .

Wrinkled, bearded,
    Clothes outgrown,
Back in town
    He's hardly known;
Lack of geri-
    Atric care
Traumatizes
    Rip for fair.

When he hears
    The thunder rolling
"It's them Little
    Leaguers bowling!"

Lady Chatterley's Lover
D. H. Lawrence

Poor Lady C.
    Can't come to grips
With hubby, dead
    Below the hips,
But finds the hired
    Keeper game,
A spunky type,
    Mellors by name.
A real four-letter
    Athlete he
Who fills the breach
    For Lady C.

She lives again,
    Her joy is utter:
"The greatest thing
    Since peanut butter!"

Sex is not sin
    Nor cause for shame,
Taboos and caste
    Are much to blame.

That's what your Uncle
    David said.
Well, kids, that's it —
    Now go to bed.

Jane Eyre
Charlotte Brontë

My Love behaved
    A bit erratic;
Our nuptial day
    Brought truth dramatic:
He *had* a wife,
    Mad, in an attic.

I fled! I roamed
    O'er moor and ditch.
When life had struck
    Its lowest pitch,
An uncle died
    And left me rich.

I sought my love
    Again, to find
An awful fire
    His home had mined,
Kippered his wife
    And left him blind.

Reader, guess what?
    I married him.
My cup is filled
    Up to the brim;
Now we are one,
    We play, we swim,

The power we share
    Defies all pain;
We soar above
    Life's tangled plain —
He Mr. Rochester,
    Me Jane!

Common Sense
Thomas Paine

Kings and aristocrats
    Britons may relish,
But to Americans
    Monarchs are hellish,
Draining our competence,
    Warring forever!
Let us use common sense
    Now, and endeavor
Not to conciliate
    (Since we're their betters),
But to set up our state
    Free of the fetters
Forged in another land.
    Strike the blow, brother!
Britain's our Motherland?
    Up The Wall, Mother!

Caesar's Commentaries on the Gallic Wars
Caius Julius Caesar

Omnia Gallia in tres partes divisa est . . .

Caesar cari dona militari orgi versus Belgae,
    Helvetii, Germani, Venetii, Britanni — iunemit.
"Romis glorius," sed Caesar, "Nomen me impunit!"
    Meni tridit — Vercingetorix, forin stans —
Caesar noctim sili fors ticinis nec aut.
    Ab ludi, nervi felo, Caius Julius, iubet.

A Farewell to Arms

Ernest Hemingway

Frederick Henry
    (Medic aid)
By an English
    Nurse is laid;
War-crossed lovers
    (World War I)
Find their love-life
    Just begun;

Caporetto!
    Bloody battle,
Routed soldiers
    Die like cattle,
Frederick's wounded
    Leg's a mess,
Cathy helps him
    Convalesce;

Swiss chalets
    Provide surcease,
They conclude a
    Separate peace;
Pregnant now,
    Her luck falls through —
Babe is still-born,
    She dies too . . .

War was futile,
      Vile, absurd;
"Glory" just a
      Dirty word;
Pride and Strength
      Emerged worth-while
(Plus an Ernest
      Writing style).

Cyrano de Bergerac

Edmond Rostand

Big-nosed hypochondriac
(Not de Gaulle — de Bergerac)
Swordsman with a golden tongue
Lends his knack to help a young
Soldier win Roxane, a blonde
Of whom both are mighty fond.

War breaks out. The newlywed
Joins the fray and winds up dead.
Poor Roxane finds solitude
In a convent, where she'll brood
And reread her lover's prose,
Not aware it's Cyrano's.

He, the prince of cavaliers
Visits her for fifteen years,
Gallantly dispelling gloom,
Holding high aloft his plume;
When Roxane at last gets wise
To the whole charade, he dies.

Through the falling autumn leaves
— Can you hear? — a spirit grieves:
"Chivalry is dead and past . . .
Good guys always finish last."

The Song of Hiawatha

Henry Wadsworth Longfellow

Hiawatha,
　　Culture hero,
Son of mighty
　　Mudjekeewis,
Slew the sturgeon
　　Mishe-Nahma,
Got in plenty
　　Mishe-Gaas,
Wed the arrow-
　　Maker's daughter,
Mini-skirted
　　Minnehaha.

When the White Man
　　With the musket
Came along, he
　　Bade him welcome,
Told the braves to
　　Be real friendly,
Then, canoeing,
　　Took off swiftly.

Hiawatha,
    If I told you
What your tribesmen
    Now are saying
By the shores of
    Gitche-Gumee,
You would sue me.

The Great Gatsby
F. Scott Fitzgerald

Gatsby's bashes, in the 'twenties
Wow'd the *dolce far nientes*
As they quaffed the cup of youth
(Ten parts gin and one vermouth);
Gatsby hoped to bring to bed
Old-flame Daisy, who is wed
But unhappy with her Tom,
He in turn has put the glom
On a mistress, name of Myrtle
(Now the plot gets really fertile) —
Daisy, driving yellow Stutz
Crashes, spilling Myrtle's guts;
Gatsby shields her, takes the blame,
George, her spouse, with vengeful aim
Shoots him in his natatorium.
At the grave-side *In Memoriam*
Friends (fair-weather) don't appear
(Champagne pals shun watery bier) . . .
High life fizzles out, forsooth,
Ten parts dream and one part truth.

Elegy Written in a Country Churchyard
Thomas Gray

Here lie
    Poor chaps
Whose deeds
    Perhaps
Would fill
    A tome,
Had they
    Left home.

If they'd
    Had sense
To jump
    The fence
And beat
    The odds —
They'd still
    Be clods.

A Doll's House

Henrik Ibsen

Husband treats her like a doll,
Nora's just a toy, that's all.
Comes a time when Thorwald's ill —
How to pay the doctor's bill?
For his sake, but secretly,
Nora stoops to forgery;
One of Thorwald's workers knows —
"Save my job or I'll expose!"

When he learns of Nora's plight,
Thorwald reams her out of sight!
Where she hoped he might be big,
He just proved an M.C. Pig.

Wiser now, she's set to rough it;
His forgiveness? He can stuff it.
Doll no more, she hoists her jib,
Slams the door! Joins Women's Lib.

Evangeline
Henry Wadsworth Longfellow

Acadian lovers
    Forced to flee;
Will Ev meet Gabe
    Again? *Mais oui!*
A search that drives
    Them nearly silly
Ends in a hos-
    Pital in Philly;
Now Ev's a nurse
    And Gabe's a case,
"It's you!" (Who else?)
    A brief embrace
Ere each must die
    Bereft of spouse.

There's not a dry
    Eye in the house.

The Count of Monte Cristo
Alexandre Dumas

Framed and jailed,
    For lifetime hitch,
Dantes escapes
    By clever switch—
Disguised as corpse
    Of jailmate stiff
He's bagged and flung
    Off Château d'If.

He makes it to
    A treasure isle
Of which he'd learned
    In durance vile;
Emerging rich
    Beyond all dreams,
He starts to wreak
    Revengeful schemes:

He hunts the men
    Who years ago
Gave him the works;
    He brings them low!

Tremendous wealth
    Helps one compete;
Persistence pays,
    Revenge is sweet.
The combination's
    Hard to beat.

Crime and Punishment

Fyodor Dostoyevsky

Up-tight student
    Axes pair.
Fearful, with the
    Cops aware,
Yet vainglorious,
    He won't chicken
Till by saintly
    Sonia stricken;
Then confession,
    Trial and sentence:

Eight Siberian years.
    Repentance
Floods his spirit,
    Hang-ups cease;
She will join him
    Seeking peace . . .

In that bleak
    Siberian hovel,
Watch him, Sonia,
    With that shovel.

The Hobbit (1)

J. R. R. Tolkien

Bilbo leaves his country seat
("Bag End," Hobbit-hole) to meet
Thirteen wacky dwarves, named Oin,
Kili, Ori, Bofur, Gloin,
Balin, Dwalin, Thorin, Nori,
Fili, Bombur, Bifur, Dori.

Off they go on missions brave,
Goblins grab them in a cave,
Spiders, elves, a wicked troll
Bar the passage to their goal —
Misty Mountain and its riches
Guarded by a dragon (which is
Just another stereotype
In this kind of mythic hype).

There's a magic ring, of course,
And a final show of force
Where the baddies, overthrown,
Yield the fabled Arkenstone;
Bilbo scorns it, bless his soul,
He just craves his hobbit-hole.

———

So, despite its good intention
Here's a tale that lacks invention.
Hobbits speak a stilted jargon,
Humorless; and in the bargain
There's a most egregious slur —
Not one female character!

But unless you're just a snob, it
Might be hard to kick the hobbit.

The Hobbit (2)

Hobbit-hole ("Bag End") is small,
Opening on a tube-shaped hall
Through which Bilbo is deployed.
(Are you listening, Sigmund Freud?)

Thus begins a life-long quest
Fraught with every horrid test
Man must undergo, at length
To achieve his ego-strength
And identity. The story
Teems with brilliant allegory!
Dragons, goblins, spiders, elves —
Are they not our darker selves?
Middle Earth is simply rife
With symbologies of Life:
"Misty Mount"—Parnassus? Sinai?—
View it through your fancy's fine eye;
"There and Back Again"—that's Hegel!
"Magic Ring"—perhaps a bagel?
"Thirteen dwarves"—a human clone?
Buy the book and roll your own.

Lolita
Vladimir Nabokov

Humbert gloats: his young nymphet
Is "ineffable" (and yet
Eff-able as she can get);

Twelve-year-old Lolita, kept
By this horny nympholept,
Clear across the country shlepped

In and out of cheap motels;
Humbert nibbles, squeezes, smells,
(She OD's on caramels);

At fifteen, mature and wise,
"Screw you!" tarnished Lola cries,
Running off with other guys

One of whom gets her with child;
This makes Humbert really wild
Seeing Lola thus defiled,

Gun in hand he stalks the chap,
Finds him, kills him, zap-zap-zap!
Then he beats the legal rap

By succumbing in his cell
Waiting trial. It's just as well:
He has earned his private hell.

Not for him apotheosis
In whose frog-eyed diagnosis
Life is just a *pederosis*.

Your Erroneous Zones, **W. W. Dyer;** *Alter Your Life,* **E. Fox;** *Help Yourself to Happiness*, **M. C. Maultsby;** *How to Be Awake & Alive*, **Newman and Berkowitz;** *Getting Close*, **B. Fast;** *How to Flatten Your Stomach*, **J. Everroad;** *Male Mid-Life Crisis*, **N. Mayer;** *The Deep Self*, **J. C. Lilly;** *Talk to Yourself*, **Austin-Lett & Sprague;** *The Hidden You*, **Alexander;** *Breaking Through*, **J. A. Miller;** *Self-Change*, **M. J. Mahoney, Ph.D.;** *Escape from Phoniness*, **A. J. Ungersma;** *Pulling Your Own Strings*, **W. W. Dyer;** *The Woman's Dress for Success Book*, **J. T. Molloy;** *Behavioral Kinesiology*, **J. Diamond;** *Why Don't You Love Yourself*, **M. Lucero;** *I'm Glad to Be Me*, **P. K. Hallinan;** *You're Someone Special*, **B. Narramore;** *Dynamics of the Lower Self*, **John-Roger;** *Love Yourself*, **E. Richardson;** *Hooray for Me!*, **Charlip & Moore;** *A New Self*, **James and Savary;** *Total Self Knowledge*, **E. Dichter;** *How to Make Your Life Work*, **Keyes & Burkan;** *Finding Ourselves*, **E. L. Corcoran;** *Positive Selfishness*, **Porat & Quackenbush;** *You're Not Just a Statistic*, **C. B. McCall;** *Total Mind Power*, **D. L. Wison;** *Celebrate Yourself*, **D. C. Briggs;** *You Can Make It Happen*, **L. Sperry;** *Outgrowing Self-Deception*, **Murphy & Leeds;** *You're In Charge*, **C. G. Osborne;** *The Winner's Notebook*, **T. I. Rubin;** *Super Self*, **D. Tennov;** *How to Bring Out the Magic in Your Mind*, **A. Koran;** *How to Get Control of Your Time & Your Life*, **A. Lakein;** *Feel Free*, **D. S. Viscott;** *etc., etc., etc., etc.*

The Self-Help Books

Why be backward, shy and futile?
    Here are ways to seize control,
To be forceful, even brutal
    As you elbow toward your goal!

Help yourself to new horizons,
    Read these guide-books, every one —
Full of self-assertive know-how
    They'll remake you! When you're done
With the final book, you'll thank it
    For the ego-trip; and then
Clutching your security blanket
    You can hide in bed again.

Portnoy's Complaint
Philip Roth

Alec Portnoy, none too choosey,
Went for any willing floozie;
Still a jerk in matters phallic
Alec also went for Alec.

Sex he snatched in wild adventures
Sure to jolt some readers' dentures;
Here are details, cruddy, mealy,
Blow by blow. There's nothing really
To imagination left
In this — er — *roman à cleft*.

To his shrink he spills the saga
How his Mama drove him gaga,
Slathered him with guilt and shame,
Pa did pretty much the same;
"Doctor, help me! I'm a bloke
Trapped inside a Jewish joke —
Look, I'm over thirty-eight,
Is it maybe not too late?
Can I ever hope to wrench
Out of this and be a mensch?"

Doctor scratches thoughtful chin:
"So. Now vee perhaps begin?"

The Joy of Sex
Alex Comfort

Be more exotic
In matters erotic,
 Don't be afraid that you're going too far!
Here is your guide book,
Nothing-to-hide book,
 No holds are barred — simply come as you are!

No joy's illicit,
The text is explicit,
 The taste is artistic, the poses are groovy;
And if you can't get it
At bookstores, don't fret — it
 Will soon be around at your neighborhood movie.

Lysistrata
Aristophanes

Lysistrata:
   "Wives of Greece,
Give your men
   A tàle of peace!
Till war stops
   It's nix on sex."

Though it causes
   Nervous wrecks,
It succeeds. A
   Clever ruse!
Athens, Sparta
   Sign a truce.

Shields unbuckled,
   Loins ungirt,
All enjoy their
   Just dessert —
Panhellenic
   Synergism.

There's a pretty
   Euphemism.

Sexual Behavior in the Human Male (The Kinsey Report)

Alfred C. Kinsey and others

When twelve thousand
    Candid males
Bare their very
    Private tales,
All our former
    Knowledge pales;
New light dawns on
    Sex-As-Is
With a rousing
    Cock-crow, viz:

Sex is mightier
    Than the sword!
Most men tried it,
    Few were bored,
Daily, nightly,
    Many scored.
Some were petting
    Very young,
Some in kissing
    Used the tongue,
Some personified
    A bung.

Sex is mightier
    Than the pen is!
Splendid, sordid,
    Pure, a menace,
Sad, glad, —

Anyone for tennis?

Critique of Pure Reason
Immanuel Kant

What's experience?
That which enters sense;
But the senses show
Less than what we know.

Here's the difference:
Objects and events
Neither seen nor felt
Build from what is dealt,

E.g., Intuition
(Sensible condition)
And for paradigm
Substance, space and time;

These are all combined
In conceptual mind
To emerge as "real"
Things we see and feel.

One demurrer, though:
Deep inside we know
Love for moral law
And a sense of awe
At the starry skies . . .
Do these symbolize
Faith? If that's the case,
Reason, pray make place.

Alice in Wonderland

Lewis Carroll

Holed up
　　With bunny,
Pre-teen
　　Acts funny,
Aberrations —
Hallucinations —
Wild Scenes —
Tarts, Queens —
Clearly, she
Needs therapy.

The Shih Ching
Kung-Tzu (Confucius)

Kuo Feng (Folk Songs)
    Three hundred Odes
Reflecting life
    In many modes:
The lovers' trysts,
    The soldier's strife,
The ebb and flow
    Of married life,
The farmer's chore,
    The season's moods,
The natural lore
    Of streams and woods . . .

"Read these," said Kung,
    "For insights keen,
They'll raise your heart
    And purge your spleen.
I might sum up
    Their themes and plots
In one phrase: 'Have
    No twisty thoughts.'
If in this light
    Life grows more clear,
Remember, folks,
    You read it here."

The Pilgrim's Progress
John Bunyan

Christian slogs
    Weary miles,
God's apostle,
    Orbi, urbi,

Through bogs,
    Over stiles,
A colossal
    Bunyan Derby.

Candide
Voltaire

Candide, errant anti-hero
Bats consistently for zero,
Brutal strangers cheat and flog him,
Quakes and fires and mishaps dog him
As he wanders here and yonder
With the luckless Cunégonde
Who in turn is mauled by rapists
While Candide is zonked by Papists.

Sheer disaster! Yet the victim
Quoting Master Pangloss' dictum,
"Everything is for the best"
Puts it to the harshest test,
Winding up, though out of harm,
Working on a turkey farm.

Dauntless soul! He never died;
Sanguine still and starry-eyed,
Candide lives, and he is well
In Hope Springs, where people dwell
Who appear somehow to be
Very much like you and me.

The Raven
Edgar Allan Poe

Raven lurches
In, perches
    Over door.
Poet's bleary
Query—
    "Where's Lenore?"
Creepy bird
Knows one word:
    "Nevermore."

The Bridge of San Luis Rey

Thornton Wilder

The place: Peru;
　　The time: Long gone.
A bridge of rope
　　Much traveled on
Goes crashing down;
　　Five natives die. . .
God's will or chance?
　　These five — but why?

Survivors tell
　　Each one a tale
Of hope and love
　　Joy and travail,
Whose summing up
　　Reveals no plan
To justify God's ways to man
But this: We're loved
　　Awhile, and then
Forgotten, both
　　By gods and men.

Yet when our worlds
　　Are sacrificed,
Love of itself
　　Will have sufficed.
More tenuous
　　Than willow strands,
The bridge called love
　　Unyielding stands;
Across it, life
　　And death touch hands.

80

The Deserted Village
Oliver Goldsmith

Sweet Auburn! loveliest village
Of the plain . . .

           What awful pillage
Has destroyed your fields of clover?
Wealthy landlords took them over
For their homes and haciendas,
Oh, the greedy money-lenders —
Chasing out the honest yokels
From their humble homes and locals,
And destroying all the charming
Fun that used to go with farming.

Men decay in such a setting!
So the State will soon be getting
Up the money for a rousing
Rehabilitation Housing,
A Suburban Site Renewal
Which will oust the landlords cruel
(Most of whom have quit already
For the taxes got too heady);
Then the Board of City Planners
Will convert the former manors
Into rows of low-cost rentals
Which may irk the Sentimentals
But will give a habitation
To the zooming population,
And, though short of a solution,
May delay the Revolution.

On Thermonuclear War

Herman Kahn

Countdown:
Ten military postures
Nine defense programs
Eight basic situations
Seven survival patterns
Six fallout levels
Five classes of wars
Four typical caveats
Three kinds of deterrents
Two buttons to press
One Armageddon

In that final fiery whirl-up
Here's the book with which to curl up.

The Compleat Angler
Izaak Walton

How to use a dunghill grub,
How to lure a bream or chub,
How to make a rod that whips,
And a hundred other tips—
Here are tales and hints galore
To delight you, piscator.

Long ago, these angles worked,
Creels filled up and spirits perked;
Free from care and trouble, you
Strolled with Izaak W.,
While he rapped with charm and wit
On the bait-and-tackle bit.
Ah, what sport the fish to burke!
Ere pollution did the work.

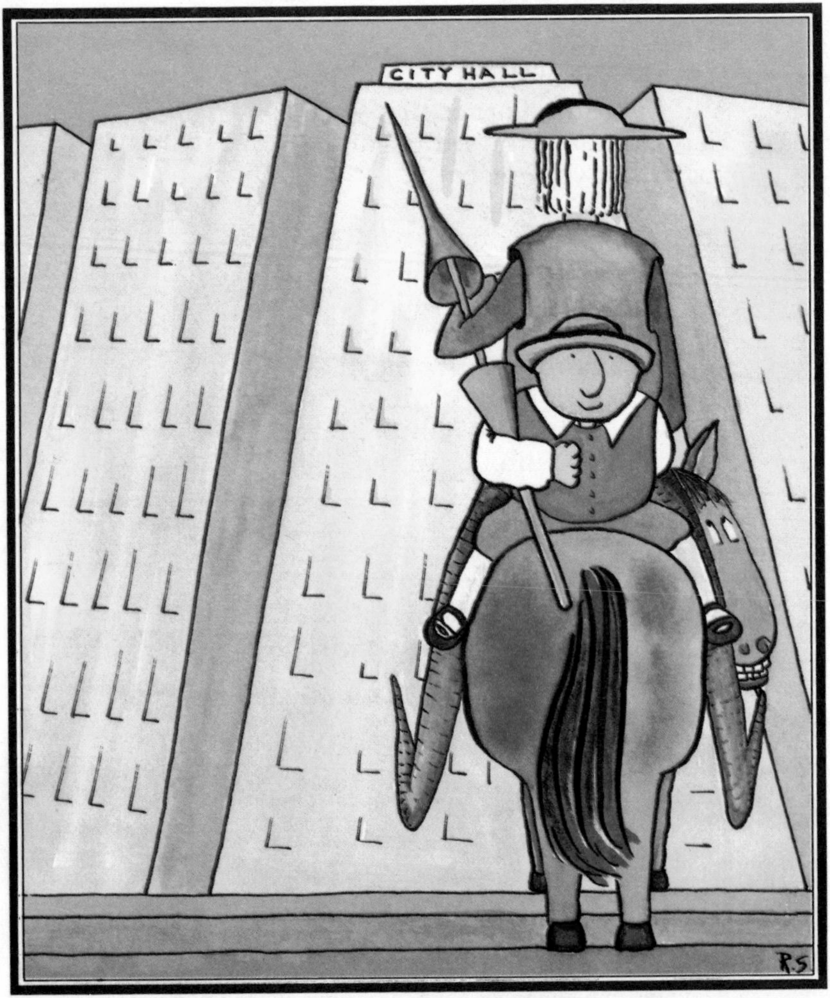
CITY HALL
R.S

Don Quixote
Miguel de Cervantes

Unhinged by tales
    Of derring-do,
This buff assails
    Injustice too;
With rusty lance,
    In armor clad,
He gallivants
    Like Galahad.

Drab peasant girls
    Are high-born dames
And windmills, giants
    (So he claims);
With foes galore
    To be subdued
He gets enor-
    Mously snafu'd.

Illusion takes
    Its awful toll
As, racked in body
    And in soul,
He dies forlorn,
    All passion spent.
Let no one scorn
    This gallant gent,

But share his poet's
    Fantasy:
"I see it as it needs must be."

Walden

Henry David Thoreau

Beyond
    Mere goods,
    The pond, the woods . . .

Live there
    As I,
    And simplify.

Reflect:
    What need?
    And check your speed.

Eschew
 The norm
 (Dull minds conform);

Two years
 Thus spent,
 I up and went

More lives
 To taste.
 Walden was cased.

Small Is Beautiful

E. F. Schumacher

This market-centered life
Breeds envy, greed and strife;
Yet those who steer our ec—
Onomic and our tech—
Nologic juggernaut
Have but one mindless thought—
"Increase the GNP!"
Now, how *gross* can you be?

Away, then, with the frauds
Of Technocratic gods!
Of Automation throned
And Giantism cloned,
Environmental rape
And man as naked ape!
Bring on creative work
That does not sap and irk,
That uses hand and brain
In projects more humane,
Not making fat cats fatter
But *as if people matter*!

On that Great Day we'll taste
A life less fouled by waste,
Conserving Nature's powers
Unsmirched by nuclear showers;
Small farms will re-appear,
And towns with rural cheer,
And hearts will join in song!

And you should live so long.

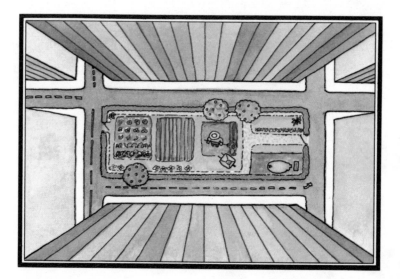

Sappho

Invocation to Sappho of Lesbos:

Of thy great verse such meager scraps remain,
To further shrink them were an act profane . . .

Singer of Love and Joy! Thou did'st impart
To Grecian maids the skills of choral art;
Wert thou to be reborn on earth today
And living in America, let's say,
In Oshkosh, Nashville, or perhaps Cos Cob,
Thou might'st be looking for a teaching job
Like that in Lesbos.

Sister, look again:
The stuff is coming down, and it ain't rain.
The righteous parents of the P.T.A.
Would rise in wrath, protesting "*She is gay!*"

Alas, Tenth Muse, thy poems and amours
Are Greek to many; yet thy fame endures.

Pygmalion
George Bernard Shaw

In Henry Higgins'
Bachelor diggins
A flower child
Is scrubbed, restyled,
From Cockney shady
To my fair lady.

It proves a whim
That pleases him;
He treats her, though,
Like clay or dough.
Winning his case,
She's left on base.

Liza's no fool.
She finds some tool
Who digs her clay
(Fred, in the play)
Marries the toff
And leaves the Prof.

Who, muttering "Traitor!"
Takes tea with Mater.

Gulliver's Travels
Jonathan Swift

In Lilliput
    He gets tied down
By tiny men
    And towed to town
Where he observes
    Their petty ways.
He doesn't find
    Too much to praise.

In Brobdignag
    Reverse the cast —
Gulliver's small,
    His captors vast.
They're rather rough,
    Their acts deride
His manliness
    And native pride.

The moral? With
    A thoughtful frown:
"Shun little guys,
    They tie you down;
If you have work
    You want to do,
Better keep clear
    Of big shots, too."

The Communist Manifesto
Karl Marx and Friedrich Engels

Workers, unite!
Workers, you knight-harassed, feudal lord-ridden
    serfs in an earlier day;
Workers, you night-toiling vassals of bourgeois
    exploiters today;
Workers, you nigh-to-death victims of class war, arise —
    grab the power away!
Workers, unite!

Quotations from Chairman Mao Tse-Tung (The "Little Red Book")

"Revolution is no party,
    It is not refined."

"Modesty is good for progress,
    Leave conceit behind."

"Men's dominion over women
    Must be undermined."

"To get rid of war and bloodshed
    We take up the gun."

"Through the force of arms and struggle
    China will be won."

"Hearken to the people's wishes,
    Try to get them done."

"In a world of social classes
    Wars will never end."

"Fight against Revisionism,
    It's a bourgeois trend."

"Let a hundred flowers blossom,
    Let all views contend!"

(Repeat)

Return of the Native
Thomas Hardy

Back to the heath
    Comes square-cut Clym;
Eustacia Vye
    Throws curves at him
While keeping Damon
    On a limb.

Her marriage doesn't
    Slow her pace.
Clym's mother calls it
    A disgrace —
"We're Egdon Heath,
    Not Peyton Place!"

Mom dies. Poor Clym
    Falls in a swound;
Eustacia, Damon
    Both get drowned.
Clym starts to preach
    When he comes round.

How Fate engulfs
    This fervid crew!
The way the author
    Spreads the grue,
The reader must be
    Hardy too.

Moby Dick or the White Whale

Herman Melville

Whale chomped Ahab's leg in two.[1]
"Hunt that beast!" he tells his crew.[2]

First, a welter of whaling schmoose,[1]
Then comes Moby and hell breaks loose.[2]

Smashup! Ahab's drowned in brine,[1]
Lashed to the whale by a harpoon line.[2]

Good (symbolic) with Evil vies,[1]
If you'd fathom it, you must rise.[2]

1. Heave ho, blow the man down!
2. Early in the morning.

The Origin of Species

Charles Darwin

All creatures strive;
The fit survive.

Out of this surge
Species emerge.

"Throw the bum out!"
Is Nature's shout,

And "Class will tell"
Sex-wise as well.

The age-old race
To win or place

(At least to show)
Persists, although

The way things look,
None dares make book.

Listen to the Warm
Rod McKuen

Are you sentimental?
    Dote on plastic charm?
Rod's massage is gentle,
    Does no lasting harm;

No deep thoughts to rile you,
Blandness to beguile you,
Pare your toenails while you
    Listen to the smarm.

The Book of Lists
David Wallechinsky, Irving Wallace and Amy Wallace

Your education may have missed
A lot of things, so here's a list
(Five hundred lists, in fact) to bring
You up to date on everything:

A list of ten non-flying birds;
The ten worst-sounding English words;
The twenty-three most boring jobs;
Ten famous gustatory slobs;
The costliest things insured by Lloyd's;
Great men who suffered hemorrhoids;
Ten people born with extra limbs;
Great writers and their pseudonyms;
Three men who perished during sex;
The ten worst automotive wrecks—

And so it goes, with list on list
To make you like an archivist,
Till groggily you wonder how
You lived without this dope till now!

Robinson Crusoe
Daniel Defoe

Wrecked castaway
    On lonely strand
Works hard all day
    To tame the land,
Takes times to pray;
    Makes clothes by hand.

For eighteen years
    His skill he plies,
Then lo! A footprint
    He espies —
"Thank God it's Friday!"
    Crusoe cries.

Take heart from his
    Example, chums:
Work hard, produce;
    Complete your sums;
Eventually,
    Friday comes.

Principles of Political Economy
John Stuart Mill

"John Stuart Mill
By a great effort of will
Overcame a natural bonhomie
And wrote the *Principles of Political Economy.*"

A quip
Too flip!
Mill's tract
In fact
has bright
Insight:

"Man's power over Nature
        should be used to shorten
        the hours of work;"

"Unproductive consumption, if it adds
        to the joy of life, may be regarded
        as a true economic surplus;"

"There is not much satisfaction in
        contemplating a world with scarcely
        a place where a wild shrub or flower
        could grow without being eradicated
        as a weed in the name of improved agriculture;"

"Money is only a medium of exchange."

For 1848
This stuff is great.

Call of the Wild

Jack London

Buck is dognapped,
    Kicked around,
Sold to roughnecks
    Klondike-bound;
He becomes a
    Tough sled hound.

Lashed by Arctic
    Cold and fog,
Blood and ice his
    Footsteps clog.
Shouldn't happen
    To a dog.

Primal urges,
    Stir his hide,
Buck becomes
    Transmogrified!
(Lassie, better
    Come inside);

Wolfish, howling,
    Man-reviled,
Scary! He will
    Drive you wild.
You should read it.
    As a child.

108

The Canterbury Tales
Geoffrey Chaucer

Whan that Aprille with his shoures sote
—In April, when it's muddy underfoot—
Than longen folk to goon on pilgrimages
—Then folks go off to spend their hard-earned wages—

(The older language has an evocation
That loses just a little in translation,
Perhaps you noticed?) Anyhow, this crowd
Of pious pilgrims, Canterbury-bound,
Told tales *en route*—replete with merry stories,
Fables and folktales, satires, allegories,
Some with a moral tone and some uncouth
And raunchy, like the Miller's Tale, forsooth,
Wherein a Carpenter, a dullish blade
Is rudely cozened and a cuckold made
By Nick and Ab, a pair of city slickers
Who scheme to get into his young wife's knickers . . .
Some fun!

        Ah, Chaucer, how thou did'st refine
With style and wit the early metric line!
Endowing literature with lasting glory—
Plus the Original Traveling Salesman's Story.

The Sonnets of William Shakespeare (Numbers 1-17)

Thine eye,
Thine air,
Defy
Compare.
This prime,
Alas,
In time
Will pass.
What can
Replace
Thy man—
Ly grace?
A son—
Make one.

The Sonnets of William Shakespeare (Numbers 18-154)

The boy
  I love
Rude joy
  May prove—
He'd spark
  (No less)
My dark
  Mistress!
This much
  I know:
It's touch
  And go
When you
  Love two.